Enid Blyton's

BEDTIME STORIES

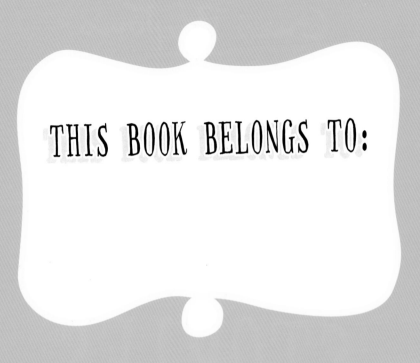

THIS BOOK BELONGS TO:

This edition published in 2014 by Bounty Books,
a division of Octopus Publishing Group Ltd
Endeavour House,
189 Shaftesbury Avenue,
London WC2H 8JY
www.octopusbooks.co.uk

An Hachette UK Company
www.hachette.co.uk

ENID BLYTON ® Text copyright ©2014 Hodder & Stoughton Ltd
Illustrations copyright © 2014 Octopus Publishing Group Ltd
Layout copyright © 2014 Octopus Publishing Group Ltd

Illustrated by Alison Winfield

ISBN: 978-0-75372-787-4

A CIP catalogue record for this book is available from the British Library

Printed and bound in China

Enid Blyton's

BEDTIME STORIES

FOR CHILDREN

Bounty Books

The Stories

1

The Adventures
of the Toy Ship

Illustrated by Alison Winfield

Mary and Timothy had a little ship. It had a fine blue sail, and its name *Lucy Ann* was painted on the side. The children often took it down to the stream to sail it, and it floated beautifully. It didn't turn over on its side as so many toy boats do – it sailed upright, just like a proper boat.

One day when Mary and Timothy were sailing the *Lucy Ann*, the string broke.

Oh dear! Down the stream it floated, faster and faster, and the children ran after it. But the little boat kept to the middle of the stream and, no matter how they tried, the children could not reach it.

At last they could no longer run by the stream, for someone's big garden ran right down to the edge of the water, and a fence stood in their way. Very sad, the children watched as the *Lucy Ann* disappeared around a bend in the stream. They went back home, afraid that their ship would feel very lost without them.

So it did. The little ship tried its hardest
to go back, but the stream took it along
too fast. On and on it went until at last
it came to rest beside a mossy bank.
Its prow stuck into the soft earth
and there it stayed. The
little ship could move
neither backwards
nor forwards.

Night came, and the ship was astonished to
see the moon in the sky, for before it had
always spent the night in the toy cupboard.
It did not know that there were such
things as moon or stars. It stared up at
the big silver moon and thought
it was very beautiful.

Then suddenly, through the silence of the night there came the sound of singing. On the opposite side of the stream, the little ship was surprised to see a great many twinkling lights, like tiny Japanese lanterns, shining in rainbow colours through the darkness.

It heard a lot of little voices, and saw a great number of fairy folk, all most excited. They were dressed in beautiful costumes – rose petal waistcoats edged with diamond dewdrops, daffodil skirts and bluebell waistcoats.

Then, as the little boat watched in amazement, a ring of toadstools sprang up, and the pixies laid little white cloths on them for tables. They set out plates and glasses, and tiny knives and forks. Then they put out some tiny golden chairs for a group of pixies who carried musical instruments.

These must be the fairy folk that Mary and Timothy sometimes talked about, thought the ship to itself. Then it saw a small boat, smaller than itself, on the opposite side of the stream, and a pixie-man got into it.

Quite nearby, on the top of its own mossy bank, the ship saw more fairy folk. They had with them all sorts of good things to eat! Honey cakes, flower biscuits, blue jellies with pink ice cream on the top, lemonade made of dew, special blancmanges in the shape of birds and animals, and many other good things.

They carried these goodies in woven baskets and on silver dishes. They were waiting for the other little boat to fetch them across the stream, so that they might lay out their food on the ring of toadstool tables.

"Hey! Little boat, come and fetch us!" they cried to the boat on the other side. The pixie-man in it began to row across. But suddenly a great fish popped up its head and made such a large wave that the pixie boat was filled with water and sank!

Oh, what a noise there was!
How all the little folk shouted
and cried in fear, when they
saw their boat sink, and the
pixie-man in the water!

"Oh, no! The boat's sunk! Oh, look at the boatman, is he safe? Oh, what shall we do now! We haven't another boat and all our lovely food is on the other side of the stream!"

Listening in dismay, the *Lucy Ann* suddenly had a grand idea! It could take the pixies to the other side, with all their baskets and dishes! So it spoke up in its funny, watery voice. How all the fairy folk jumped when they heard it! One little pixie was so surprised that she dropped the dish she was carrying, and spilt blue jelly all over the grass.

"I will take you across the stream, if you know how to sail me," said the little ship. "Don't be frightened. I am only a toy ship, I cannot hurt you. I will be only too glad to be of help."

The pixies ran to the little ship and chattered at the tops of their silvery voices. Yes, it would do beautifully! What luck that it happened to be there! If it hadn't, the party would have been spoilt – and the King and Queen themselves were coming!

Soon, the pixies had loaded all their food on board and settled down. One of them sat at the front and guided the ship out into the moonlit stream.

How proud the little toy ship was! Never before had it had anything but dolls aboard, and they couldn't do anything but sit still and stare at the sky. But these little fairy folk chattered and laughed. They ran here and there across its decks, they leaned over the side and tried to dip their fingers in the water. It was great fun for the little ship!

Out it went over the stream, sailing most beautifully. The wind filled its sails and it floated like a swan, proud and handsome.

The fairies on the other side cried out in delight – they were so grateful that the *Lucy Ann* had saved their party. And would you believe it, at that very moment the King and Queen of Fairyland arrived, riding in their golden carriage!

They watched the little boat too, and how
pleased they were to see it come safely to
the bank. All the fairies cheered, and the
ship's blue sail trembled with joy.

The *Lucy Ann* stayed by the bank to watch the party. It smiled to see the little folk dancing to their pixie music.

And then the King and Queen asked the little ship if it would take them for a sail up the stream in the moonlight. What an honour!

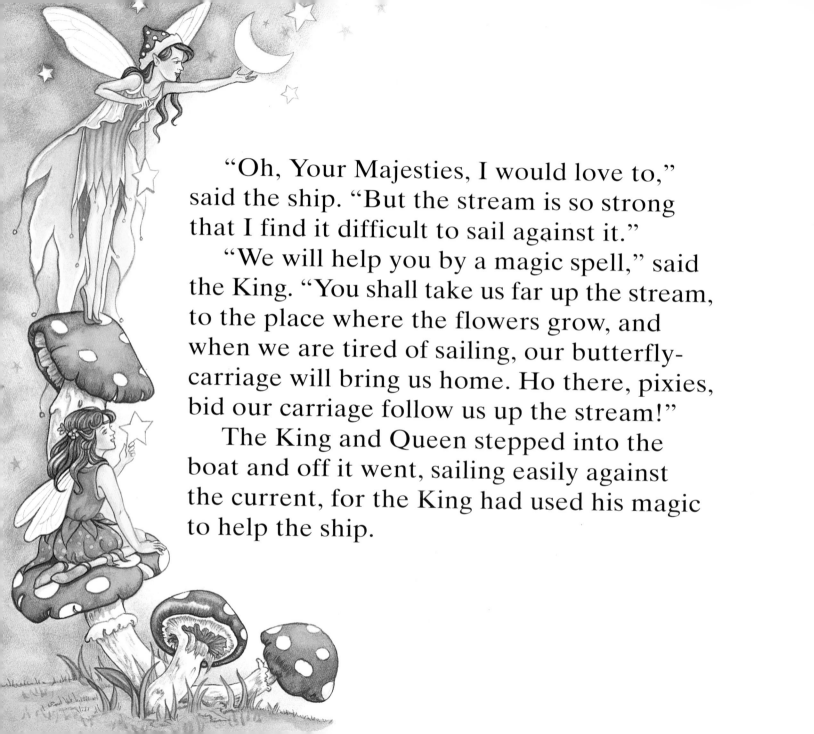

"Oh, Your Majesties, I would love to," said the ship. "But the stream is so strong that I find it difficult to sail against it."

"We will help you by a magic spell," said the King. "You shall take us far up the stream, to the place where the flowers grow, and when we are tired of sailing, our butterfly-carriage will bring us home. Ho there, pixies, bid our carriage follow us up the stream!"

The King and Queen stepped into the boat and off it went, sailing easily against the current, for the King had used his magic to help the ship.

How enjoyable it was, sailing along in the moonlight! The little ship had never felt so happy or so proud – after all, it was carrying the King and Queen of Fairyland.

It was a beautiful night. On either side, the banks were lined with trees that shone silver in the moonlight, and the little waves on the stream looked like silver, too.

Bats fluttered silently overhead and the old owl hooted to them as he flew by. All around them the little ship fancied it could hear the sound of fairy voices, singing a gentle lullaby. It was a most exciting journey.

After a lovely long sail the King spoke to the little ship once more.

"We will land now," he said. "Draw in to the bank, little ship. See where our butterfly carriage awaits us!"

The ship saw a beautiful carriage drawn by four yellow butterflies. It was waiting by a fence on the bank, overhung with beautiful roses.

The *Lucy Ann* sailed to the side and waited there while the King and Queen got out. Then, as it looked about, the little ship gave a glad cry.

"Why! This is where Mary
and Timothy played with
me this morning!" it said.
"If only I could stay here,
then they might find me
in the morning!"

"Of course you shall stay here," said the King. "I will tie you to a stick."

So he tied the little ship tightly to a twig in the bank. The King then said goodbye and thanked the ship very much for all its help.

"I will turn your sail into a silver one, in reward for your kindness," said the Queen. In a trice the ship's blue sail became one of glittering silver thread. It was really splendid. Then the King and Queen mounted their butterfly carriage and off they rode in the moonlight.

Soon it was dawn.
The ship slept for a
little while, and then
woke up. It was proud
of its glittering silver
sail, and it longed for
Mary and Timothy to
come down to the
stream to see it.

The children came running down before breakfast – and how they stared when they saw the little toy ship!

"Look at that beautiful ship!" cried Mary. "Where did it come from? It's just like ours, only it has a silver sail!"

"I wonder who tied it to that stick," said Timothy, puzzled. "Nobody comes down here but us."

"Ooh, look, Timothy – it *is* our ship! It's called *Lucy Ann*!" cried Mary, in excitement. "See, its name is on the side so it *must* be ours. But how did it get its beautiful sail, and who tied it up here for us to find!"

"The fairies must have had a hand in it," said Timothy. "And see, Mary – this proves it! Look at those two tiny cakes on the deck there! The fairies used our ship last night, and one of them dropped those cakes! Did you ever see such tiny things!

Shall we eat them?"
"Yes – but let's save them till
tonight, then maybe we'll
see the fairies too!" cried Mary.
They took their ship
from the water and ran
to tell Mummy all
about it. She was so
surprised to see its
silver sail!

The ship was glad to be back in the toy cupboard. And how it enjoyed itself telling all the other toys of its adventures!

Mary and Timothy are going to eat those pixie cakes tonight. I do wonder what will happen, don't you?

2

The
Magic Sweetshop

Illustrated by Alison Winfield

Jo and Tom were going over Breezy Hill for a walk when they saw a narrow path going off to the west that they had never seen before.

"Hallo!" said Tom, in surprise. "I've never seen that path before. Let's see where it leads, shall we, Jo?" So off they went down the funny little path. Little did they know that it was to be the beginning of a very strange adventure!

After a while they came to what looked like a tiny village – just three or four cottages set closely on the hillside with two little shops in the middle. One of them was a funny little shop with a small window of thick glass. Behind the panes were tall, thin bottles of brightly coloured sweets.

"A sweet shop," said Jo, surprised. "I didn't know there was one on this hill, did you, Tom?"

"No," said Tom. Jo pressed her nose to the window and looked at the bottles of sweets.

She cried out in surprise as she read their labels.
   "Tom! These are very strange sweets! Just
read what they are!" Tom looked at the labels,
and certainly the names of the sweets were very
strange indeed. The blue sweets were labelled
Giant-sweets, and the pink ones Dwarf-sweets.
There were lots of other kinds too.

"You know, this must be a magic shop," said Jo, excitedly. "Let's go in and buy some! I've got a penny and so have you."

So they pushed open the door and went inside. At first they thought there was nobody there, but then they saw a small nobbly-looking man sitting behind the counter. He was wearing a pair of large spectacles on his long nose.

He had a strange tuft of hair growing straight up from his head and two long, pointed ears. He was sitting by himself reading a bright-blue newspaper.

"What would you like this morning?" he asked, folding up his newspaper neatly.

"Could we have a pennyworth of mixed sweets each?" asked Tom, eagerly.

"Certainly!" said the shopman, twitching his pointed ears like a dog. He took four bottles from the window and emptied some sweets onto his scales. Jo looked at the labels on the bottles so that she would know which of the sweets were which. She saw him place a Giant-sweet, a Dwarf-sweet, an Invisible-sweet, and a Home-Again-sweet into the scales.

The children felt very much excited when the shopman handed each of them a bag. He took their pennies and put them into a tin box. Then he picked up his blue newspaper and began to read again.

"What will happen to us if we eat these sweets?" Tom asked the little man, but all he would say was,

"Try, and see!"

The children didn't like to ask him anything else so they went outside and walked up the little crooked street. They were surprised when they came to a big white gate that went right across the road.

"This is stranger and stranger," said Tom.

"I've never seen that village before, and now here is a gate that I've never seen before either."

"Shall we climb over?" said Jo. "We are nearly at the top of the hill."

"Yes, let's," said Tom. To their great surprise, they saw a town on the other side!

"How strange!" said Jo. "There has never been anything on the other side of this hill before!"

They went on down towards the town, and soon met some most peculiar-looking people. They were very round, and their arms were very long indeed. Their faces were as red as tomatoes and they wore big white ruffs round their necks, which made their faces seem redder than ever.

Some of them were riding in small motor cars, rather like toy ones but with hoods like sunshades instead of proper hoods. Jo and Tom stood in the middle of the road and stared in astonishment.

A motor car with a bright-yellow hood came along at a tremendous pace. Tom jumped to one side, but Jo was just too late and the little car ran right into her. To her great amazement it exploded in to a hundred pieces!

The little round man in the car shot up in the air and down again. He landed on the ground with a bump and he *was* cross!

"You silly, stupid, foolish, ridiculous girl!" he cried. "Why didn't you get out of my way? Look what you've done to my car? It's gone pop!"

"Well," said Jo, getting up. "I'm sorry, but you were driving too fast. You didn't even hoot."

"You horrid, nasty, rude, selfish girl!" cried the little man, getting even crosser.

"Hey!" said Tom. "Don't speak to Jo like that! Haven't you any manners? You might have hurt her very much running into her like that!"

The little round man went quite purple with rage. He took a trumpet from his pocket and blew loudly on it. "Tan-tara! Tan-tara!"

At once a whole crowd of funny-looking people came running up and took hold of Jo and Tom.

"Take them to prison!" shouted the man
whose motor car had exploded. "Give them
nothing but bread and water for sixty days!"

The children could do nothing against so many, so they were marched off to a big yellow building and locked up in a tiny cell. Tom banged on the door but it was no use. It was locked and bolted on the outside.

"Look here, Jo!" said Tom, suddenly. "Let's eat one of these sweets each. Perhaps something will happen to help us!"

So they each picked from their bags a blue sweet and put it into their mouths. And before long a very curious thing happened! They began to grow taller. Yes, and fatter, too! In fact their heads soon touched the ceiling.

"I say! Those must have been the sweets out of Giant-sweet bottle!" said Tom, in excitement.

He kicked at the door and it almost broke, for his feet were now very big.
"Stop that!" cried an angry voice outside. "If you kick your door again, prisoners, I shall not give you any supper!"

"Ho!" said Tom, pleased. "I shall certainly kick it again! Then when it's opened, Jo, we'll walk out and give everyone a shock!"

"Bang, bang, bang!" He kicked the door hard again. At once it was unbolted and unlocked and a very angry keeper came in. But when he saw how big the children were, his red face turned quite pale and he ran away as fast as his little legs would carry him!

Tom and Jo squeezed out of the door and went down the street. How they laughed to see the astonishment on the faces of the townsfolk, who now looked very small indeed.

Soon they came to a crossroads. There was a signpost, and on it was printed, "To Giantland."

"Goodness!" said Jo. "How exciting! We are giants now Tom. Do let's take this road and see if we can find some other giants."

So the children set off, feeling more and more excited. After half-an-hour they came to some enormous trees and realised that they must have arrived in Giantland.

Soon after that they saw a giant – but dear me, the giants were far bigger than the children had guessed they would be! In fact, they were enormous! They towered over the children.

A very large giant with eyes like dinner plates saw them first. He gaped at Tom and Jo in surprise and then called to his friends nearby in a voice like thunder.

"HEY! LOOK HERE! HERE ARE SOME STRANGE CHILDREN!"

In a trice the children were surrounded by a dozen huge giants. They didn't like it at all. One of the giants poked his finger into Tom's chest.

"He's real," he said, in a booming voice. "He's not a doll."

"Of course I'm not a doll!" shouted Tom, crossly. "Don't poke me like that!"

It amused the giants to see how cross Tom was, and they poked him again and again with their big, bony fingers.

"Aren't they nasty, unkind creatures," cried Jo, for she didn't like the great giants with their enormous eyes and teeth like piano-keys.

"Oh, Tom. Can't we escape?"
cried Jo.

"How can we?" said
Tom, trying to push away
a finger that came to tickle him.

"Oh, I know Jo! Let's eat another sweet!"
In a great hurry the children took out their
sweet bags and ate a pink sweet each. In an
instant they felt themselves growing smaller and
smaller – smaller and smaller. The giants seemed

to grow bigger and BIGGER and BIGGER. Soon they were so big that they seemed like mountains! The children were tinier than sparrows to the giants – tinier than ladybirds even!

"Quick!" said Jo, catching hold of Tom's hand. "Let's go somewhere safe before they tread on us!"

There was a large hole in the ground not far from them and Jo and Tom ran to it. It seemed like a dark tunnel to them, but really it was a wormhole!

Down the tunnel they went, meeting huge worms and other giant creatures as they went. A great beetle hurried by them, treading heavily on Jo's toes. It was all rather alarming.

"I wish we could get out of here," said Tom, after a time. "Oh look, Jo! There's a tiny pinhole of light far ahead of us. That must be where the wormhole ends. Come on!"

On they went and at last came out into the sunshine.

They were on a green hillside, and nearby was a notice which said: "Broomstick Hill. All trespassers will be turned into Snails."

"Ooh!" said Jo in alarm. "Look at that!"

But they hardly had time to read the notice before there was a strange whirring noise up above them. To the children's enormous surprise about a hundred witches came flying through the sky on broomsticks. They darkened the sky like a black cloud.

The witches were heading for the green hillside and, of course, the very first thing their sharp eyes saw was Jo, with her golden-yellow hair. Tom had hidden quickly behind a bush, but Jo was so surprised to see the witches that she hadn't even thought of hiding!

As the witches came rushing over towards them, Tom pulled Jo down beside him.

"Get out your sweet bag and eat a sweet!" he whispered. "We've got two left. Eat the purple one and we'll see what happens!"

"Where is that trespassing child!" cried the witches. "We will turn her into a snail! How dare she come to our hillside!"

Jo and Tom popped the purple sweets into their mouths. They looked around – and to their surprise they couldn't see each other. At first they didn't know what had happened, and then they guessed – the sweets had made them invisible!

The children ran off down the hill. When they looked back at the witches, they were hunting in astonishment all around the bush where they had seen Jo.

"There's no one here!" they cried. "Where has she gone?"

By this time Jo and Tom were at the bottom of the hill. As they could not see one another, they held each others hands very firmly.

"I'm tired of this adventure," said Jo, at last. "We always seem to be chased by something – funny people, or giants, or witches. Goodness knows what it will be next time! Can't we go home now, Tom?"

"But we don't know the way," said Tom, looking around. "I'm hungry and I'd love to go home. I wish I *did* know the way! However are we going to get home again, Jo?"

"I know," said Jo, feeling for her sweet bag. "Let's eat the last sweet shall we, Tom, and see what happens."

So the children put their last sweet – a red one – into their mouths and before they had finished eating it they could see one another again! They were so pleased, for they were both tired of being invisible!

Tom and Jo waited patiently to see what else would happen. Would a big wind come and carry them home? Or perhaps a fairy carriage pulled by butterflies would arrive to help them. They waited and waited, but nothing happened. They looked at each other and sighed.

Jo and Tom just went on sitting there at the bottom of the hill, waiting in the sunshine. But still nothing happened. It was very strange.

Perhaps the Home-again sweets wouldn't take them home after all? If not, how would they get there? They were quite sure they would never be able to find the way by themselves!

Then Jo began to look around her. She saw a big fir tree that she seemed to know. She noticed a house not far off that looked familiar, and she was sure she recognised the pathway leading up the hill. Suddenly she jumped up with a cry of delight.

"Tom! We *are* home! This is the hill just outside our own garden! That's our house over there! Why, we've been home all the time and didn't know it! However could we have got here! I'm sure the hill outside our garden isn't really a witch's hill."

They were most astonished, but it was quite true – they *were* home again. They were just outside their own garden. They could see their mother standing at the front door.

"Well, how surprising!" said Tom, standing up and brushing himself down. "We're safely back after our adventures. Let's go and tell mother. Perhaps she'll come with us this evening and see that funny sweet shop on the hillside."

The children ran home and told their mother all about their strange adventures. That evening they all went up the hillside to find the sweet shop. They followed the little path – but alas, it did not lead to a sweet shop at all; only to a great many rabbit holes!

"It's just a rabbit path!" said mother. "You must have dreamed it all, my dears!"
But they didn't really, you know!

3

Whiskers
and the Wizard

Illustrated by Alison Winfield

There was once a wizard called Blunder. He was the youngest and smallest of all the wizards, and he was not very good at learning magic.

He made so many mistakes that all the other wizards laughed at him.

"One of these days you'll cast a magic spell on yourself by mistake," they said, "and then you'll be in a fine pickle!"

But Blunder wouldn't listen to any advice. He thought he knew everything.

He carried on making spells, stirring up strange recipes for magic in his boiling cauldron, and muttering enchanted words to himself. He had one servant – a faithful little rabbit called Whiskers. Most wizards, like witches, have cats for servants, for cats are wise and can keep secrets. But magic cats cost a great deal of money and Blunder couldn't afford one. So he had a rabbit instead, which was much cheaper.

Whiskers was a very clean and tidy servant. He swept and dusted, cooked and mended and looked after Blunder very well indeed. Sometimes he stirred the cauldron himself, though he was afraid of what magic might come out of it.

When he saw that Blunder often made mistakes, he was worried in case the little wizard should harm himself. He was very fond of his master, and wouldn't have let anything happen to him for all the world. So one day Whiskers asked if he could look at all the magic books. That way he thought he might learn some magic himself, and perhaps be able to help Blunder one day. But Blunder just laughed at him.

"Why, you're only a rabbit!" he said. "You'll

never be able to learn any magic. But you can look at my magic books if you like."

So Whiskers waited until his work was done. Then he took down the magic books one by one, and read them all. He had a good memory, and very soon he knew a great many spells, and could say hundreds of magic words.

One day he saw Blunder mixing spiders' webs, blue mushrooms and the yolk from a goose's egg, chanting as he went,

"Tick-a-too, fa-la-lee,
Ta-ra, ta-ra, ta-roo,
Dickety, hickety, jiminy-japes,
Bibble and scribble and boo!"

"Master! Master!" cried Whiskers, dropping his broom in a hurry. "You're saying the wrong words! Instead of making magic to grow a goose that lays golden eggs, you are saying a spell that will turn you into a goose yourself!"

It was true! Blunder had made a mistake. Already feathers had begun to sprout from his shoulders! Hurriedly he began to chant the right spell, and the feathers slowly disappeared.

But instead of being grateful to Whiskers, he was cross with him!

"I'd soon have found out my mistake!" he said sharply. "Get on with your work, Whiskers, and in future don't interfere in things that you know nothing about."

The next day, the powerful Wizard of Woz came to tea, but he arrived with bad news.

"The wicked goblin has been seen again in Pixie Wood," said the old wizard. "So we want *you* to get rid of him, Blunder. Or better still, make

some magic that will get him into our power. Then we can make him into a useful servant. You know how to do it, don't you?"

"Of course I do!" said Blunder.

"You can trust me to do a simple thing like that! The goblin will be in your power before midnight."

Blunder set to work as soon as the wizard had
gone. He mixed together green elderberries,
a small moonbeam, two thorns from a
blue rose, and a drop of honey.
Then he had to count from
ninety-nine back to one,
and stir all the time
from left to right.

"Ninety-nine, ninety-eight, ninety-seven," began Blunder and he had almost got to twenty, when Whiskers gave a cry of fear.

"Master! You're stirring the wrong way! Oh dear, oh dear, you'll put yourself in the goblin's power, instead of getting him into yours!"

Blunder stopped stirring in fright and began stirring the other way – but you can't do that sort of thing in the middle of a powerful spell! Something is bound to happen, and all of a sudden it did! There was a tremendous BANG and a blue-green flame shot out of the cauldron and whizzed twice around the room. Then it turned into a swirling purple wind that whisked Blunder up into the air and out of the window!

Whiskers crouched in a corner and waited for something else to happen. But nothing did – except that he heard a very strange laugh from somewhere that made him shiver and tremble.

"That was the goblin!" thought the little rabbit. "He knows that Blunder has put himself in his power, and he's come to get him. Oh dear, I must try to rescue him at once!"

Meanwhile Blunder had flown out of the window, risen as high as the clouds, and then come down, bump, in a place he didn't know!

"This is a fine thing!" he said. "Now what am I to do?" But at that moment he heard a horrid laugh, and suddenly there in front of him stood the wicked little goblin.

"Ho ho!" said the goblin. "Now you're in *my* power, Blunder. You don't deserve to be a wizard when you make such silly mistakes. Come along, I'm going to keep you in my cave and you can be my servant!"

"Never!" cried Blunder. "I won't go."

But the goblin knew a little magic too. He muttered a few strange words, and at once Blunder's feet began to walk in the direction that the goblin wished them to.

"You will stay here until I get back," said the wicked goblin when they had reached his cave. "And just in case you try to misbehave, this will stop you."

He drew a white chalk circle right around poor Blunder who watched him in dismay, for he knew that the circle was a magic one and would stop him using any spells to escape.

"Please set me free," Blunder begged.

But the goblin would not listen. He just clapped his hands seven times, laughed and disappeared. At the same time a great stone rolled over the entrance to the cave, leaving Blunder all alone in the cold and dark.

"No one but Whiskers knows I am gone!" he wept. "And how will he be able to help me? He's only a silly little rabbit."

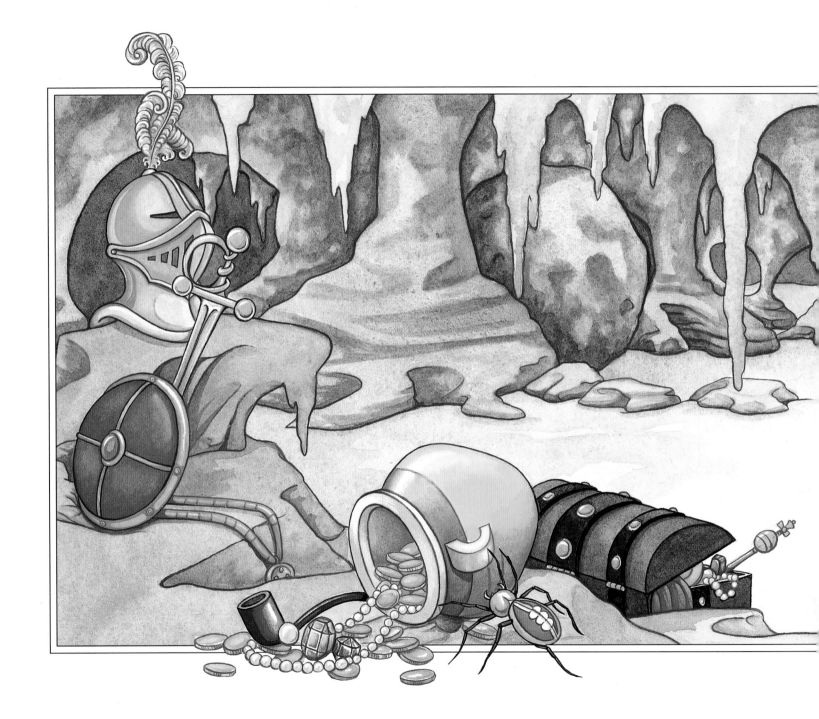

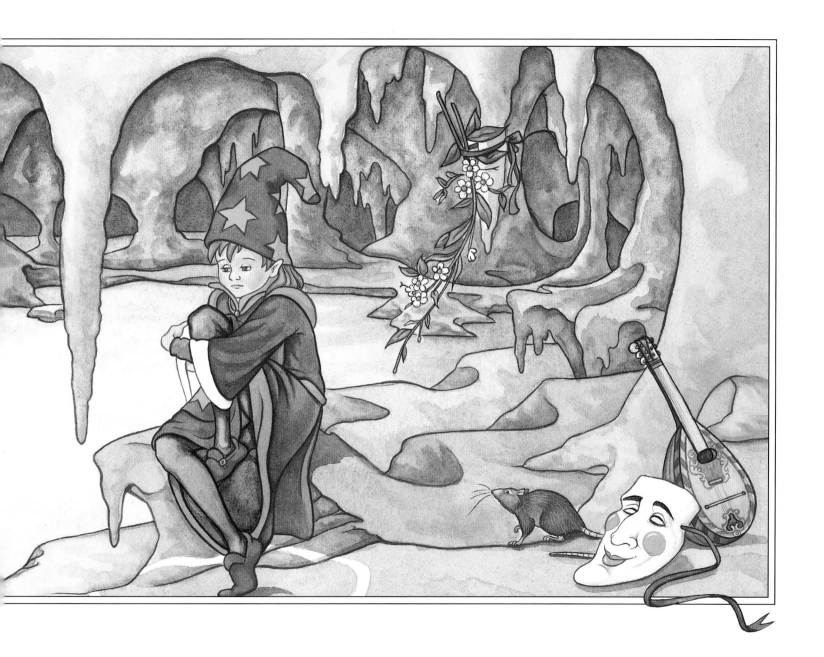

Little did Blunder know that at that very moment Whiskers was busy searching for him. He had just reached the edge of Goblin Land and was trying to decide which way to go first.

"Now what I need is that spell I read the other day," muttered Whiskers to himself. "That will help me find my master."

Soon he had remembered what to do. He took five green leaves and put them in a circle with their ends touching. Then he found a white feather and blew it into the air, singing the magic words as he did so. When he looked down again, the leaves had vanished! But the feather was still floating in front of him, floating away to the west as if blown by a strong breeze.

"Lead me to my master!"
cried the rabbit, and followed
the feather as it danced off
down the hillside.

Soon it brought Whiskers to the cave. As soon as the little rabbit saw the great stone at the entrance he felt certain that his master was imprisoned behind it.

"Master, Master!" he called out. "Are you there? It's me, Whiskers." Inside the cave, Blunder could not believe his ears.

"Oh, Whiskers, is it really you!" he cried. "I have been trapped in here by the wicked goblin. Can you help me escape? Can you move the stone?"

But even though Whiskers pushed against the great stone with all his strength; he could not move it even one inch.

"Never mind," said the little wizard, in despair. "Even if you could move it, it wouldn't be much use, for I can't move out of this magic circle. And even if I knew how to do that, I can't remember the spell that would get rid of the goblin's power."

"Perhaps I can help," cried the little rabbit. "I think I can remember the spell about goblins." And he started to recite it carefully to Blunder.

"That's just the one I want!" cried Blunder. "Oh, Whiskers! If only you could gather all the ingredients together, I might be able to escape. But I'm afraid it's quite impossible."

"Why's that?" said Whiskers in dismay.

"Because the final ingredient is a hair from my head," explained Blunder. "So unless we can move this stone, I'm stuck. I shall have to be that horrid goblin's slave forever."

Whiskers pushed at the great stone again, but it was no use. Then he had a brilliant idea! Wasn't he a rabbit? Couldn't he burrow like all rabbits do?

At once he began to burrow
into the hillside, just beside the
cave entrance. He sent out the
earth in great showers, and
in minutes he had made a
tunnel into the cave
where Blunder sat.

"Hurray!" cried Blunder. "You're quite the most brilliant rabbit in the whole world. Now we can get to work."

The little wizard knew that the one thing that could destroy the goblin's power was the sight of a red, frilled dragon. And the spell told them exactly how to make one. So all that day and all that night brave little Whiskers went in and out of his tunnel, fetching nightshade berries, white feathers, blue toadstools, sunbeams, moonbeams and everything else that Blunder needed.

Soon all the ingredients were neatly piled at one end of the enormous cave. Whiskers put the last one on the very top and then sat down with his master to wait for the goblin to return.

Early the next morning they heard the goblin outside the cave. He shouted a magic word, and the stone flew away from the entrance. Then he strode in. Whiskers had hidden himself, and Blunder was pretending to be asleep.

"Ho ho! Ha ha!" said the goblin. "What about a nice hot breakfast, Blunder? You must be hungry by now."

The wizard pretended to groan.

"Well, tell me a few secret spells and I will give you some toast and eggs," said the goblin.

"Here is one," said Blunder, raising his head, and he began to chant the spell that would turn all the magic things at the end of the cave into a fearful frilled dragon! The goblin listened carefully, grinning all the while because he thought that he was hearing a wonderful new spell.

Then, just as Blunder got to the last words, a strange thing happened. A rushing, swishing noise came from the end of the cave, and suddenly a dreadful bellow rang out. Then two yellow eyes gleamed, and lo and behold! A great dragon came rushing out!

"A frilled dragon!" yelled the goblin in fright. "Oh my! Oh my! A great, red frilled dragon! Let me out! Let me go!"

And the goblin leapt six feet into the air, turned into a puff of smoke, and streamed out of the cave with the dragon after him. Whiskers and Blunder followed, and the last they saw of the wicked goblin was a thin cloud of smoke way up in the eastern sky.

The dragon soon gave up the chase,
and turned back towards the cave.
"Quick!" whispered Whiskers.
"Change him into something
else or he will eat us too!"

Blunder clapped his hands twice, and uttered a command. The dragon began to shrink, and when it was as small as a football it turned into a mass of red flames.

Whiskers hurriedly filled a jug with water and gave it to Blunder, who threw it over the flames – and sizzle-sizzle-sizzle, they went out! Nothing was left of the frilled dragon except for a few wet ashes.

"My goodness," said Blunder, sitting down on the ground with a sigh. "We have been having too many adventures, Whiskers. I shall be glad to get home, and sleep in my soft bed!"

"Poor Master, you must be very tired," said the kind rabbit. "Jump up on my back, and I'll take you home before you can say 'Tiddley-winks'!"

So Blunder climbed up on Whiskers' soft back, and very soon he was safely home.

"Thank you very much for all you have done for me," said the little wizard, hugging the delighted rabbit. "I think you are much cleverer than I am, Whiskers."

"From now on you shall be my partner, not my servant, and you shall wear a pointed hat like me! We will do all our spells together, and then perhaps I shan't ever make a mistake again!"

Whiskers was so pleased.

"Well, let's go to bed now and have some sleep," said Blunder, yawning. "I can hardly keep my eyes open. Then tomorrow, we will go and buy your pointed hat." So they both fell asleep, and Whiskers dreamed happily of wearing a pointed hat and helping Blunder with his spells.

Many years have passed since Blunder had his adventure with the wicked goblin. Whiskers is still with him, but now Blunder is very old, and Whiskers' ears have gone grey with age.

Sometimes when all their work is done, they sit one on each side of the fireplace, and Whiskers says: "Do you remember that time when you made a mistake in your spells?"

Then they both laugh loudly, and wonder where the wicked goblin went to – for he has never been heard of from that day to this.